ELIZABETH
GOES CAMPING

DARLENE UNRUH

Goes Camping
Copyright © 2022 by Darlene Unruh

All rights reserved. No part of this publication may be reproduced, distributed, or transmitted in any form or by any means, including photocopying, recording, or other electronic or mechanical methods, without the prior written permission of the author, except in the case of brief quotations embodied in critical reviews and certain other non-commercial uses permitted by copyright law.

tellwell

Tellwell Talent
www.tellwell.ca

ISBN
978-0-2288-7714-1 (Hardcover)
978-0-2288-7713-4 (Paperback)

This book is dedicated to my husband, Tony, my best friend, who makes it possible for me to fulfill my dream of publishing my books, and who takes us camping.

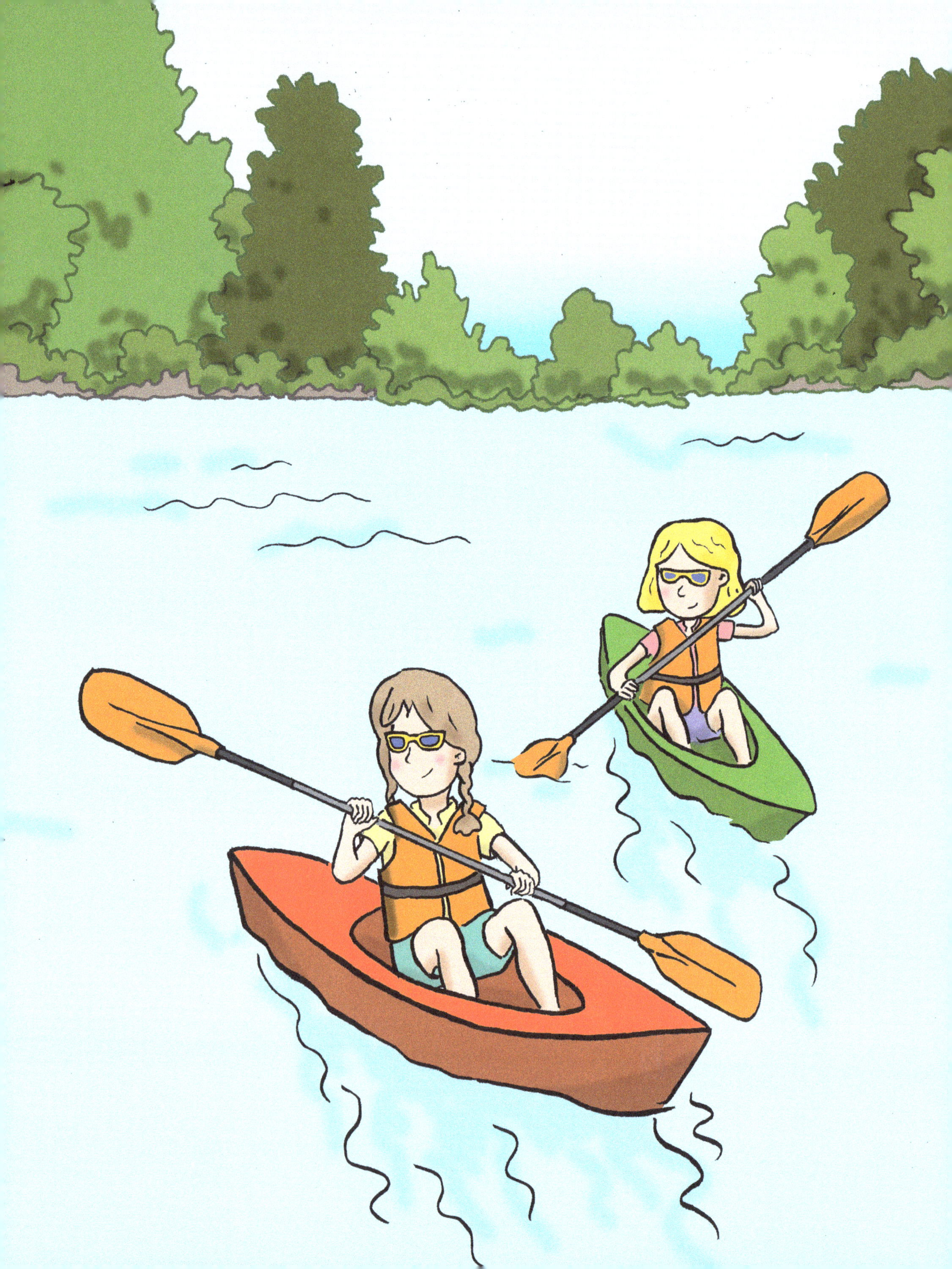

Elizabeth's kayak glided quietly through the water. Her brothers Christopher, Benjamin, and Nicholas were farther ahead. Abigail, her sister paddled alongside in her own kayak, enjoying the family outing. Dad and Mom were right behind them in a canoe, and Victoria her little sister was with them.

Elizabeth loved everything about summertime. The music of the katydids and crickets, the calls of the birds, the humming of the bees and flies, and even the occasional whining of a mosquito around her ear. The rippling water, the wind rustling in the treetops overhead. Altogether, the sounds formed the lovely song of summer—her favorite season.

Dad and Mom paddled their canoe up beside Elizabeth. They told her they were going to turn around and go back to the cabin. Victoria was getting tired and cranky. Mom would feed her and put her down for a nap in the cabin while Dad started the fire and worked on supper. In half an hour or so, he would come down to the bridge with the pickup to get the children and their kayaks. Then they would return to their campsite for supper.

Elizabeth listened to the soft, rhythmic splashing of their paddles growing fainter and fainter, as Dad and Mom paddled back upriver. Soon she couldn't hear them at all. She turned around and watched them disappear around the bend.

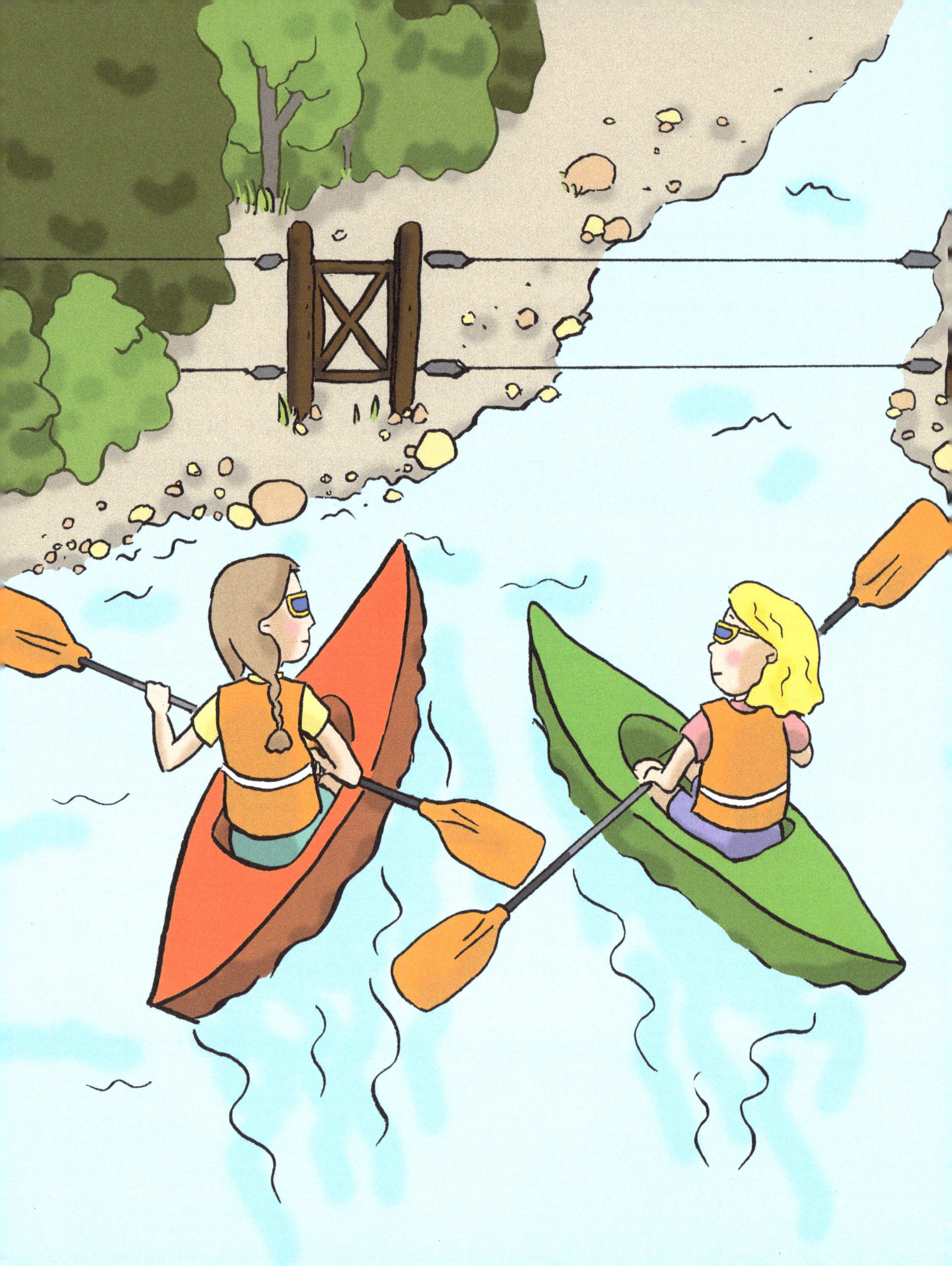

Suddenly, Elizabeth noticed there was a small puddle of water down by her feet. As she paddled, she kept her eyes on the water pooling in the bottom of her kayak. Sure enough, ever so slowly, the puddle was growing bigger. Soon, she was sitting in water.

Elizabeth found a shallow place to pull her kayak out of the water, stand it on its end, and drain it via its plug. Abigail waited in her kayak for Elizabeth to finish. Of course, it would have been easier and faster if she weren't weak and helpless with laughter. It was just too funny. How come the girls were stuck with the leaky kayak?!

Soon she and Abigail were on their way again. But before long, Elizabeth had to find another place to drain the kayak. The leak was slowing them down significantly. The boys were probably down by the bridge already, having fun swimming and jumping off the rocks.

Up ahead, they saw there was a fence stretching from one riverbank to the other.

"Now what?!" Abigail shouted to her older sister.

Elizabeth watched the fence get closer and closer.

"The boys never said anything about this fence being here," Elizabeth answered. "Maybe it wasn't here when they kayaked this part of the river last summer."

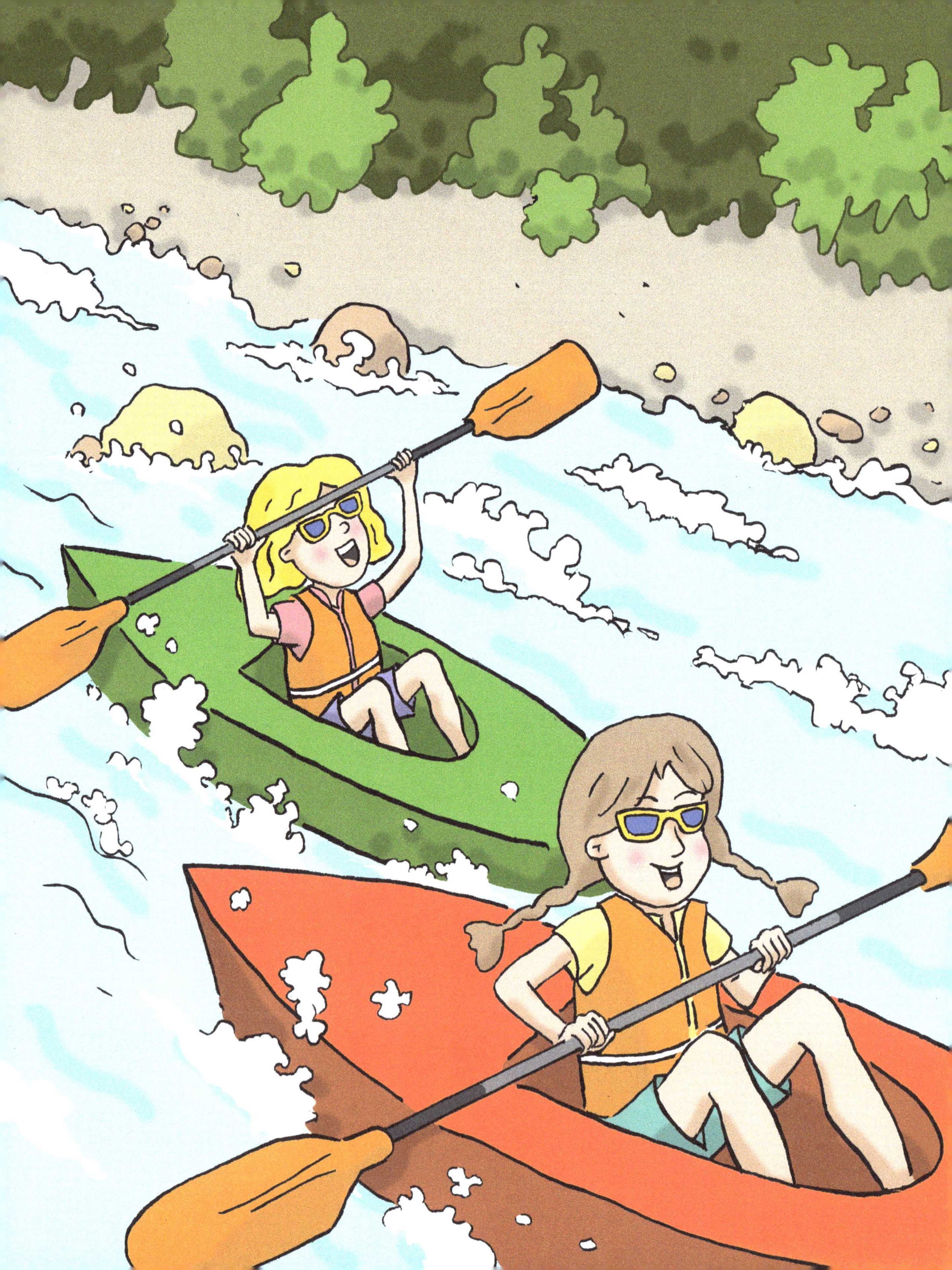

The girls each slithered down into their kayaks and drifted under the fence. When they sat up again, safely on the other side of the fence, Abigail hooted with laughter at the sight of Elizabeth. Water was dripping off her. Joining in the laughter, Elizabeth diligently searched for another place to drain the water out of her kayak.

On their way once again, both girls managed the rapids without any spills, and finally arrived at the bridge where they found the boys swimming. Abigail and Elizabeth lost no time joining the boys in the water.

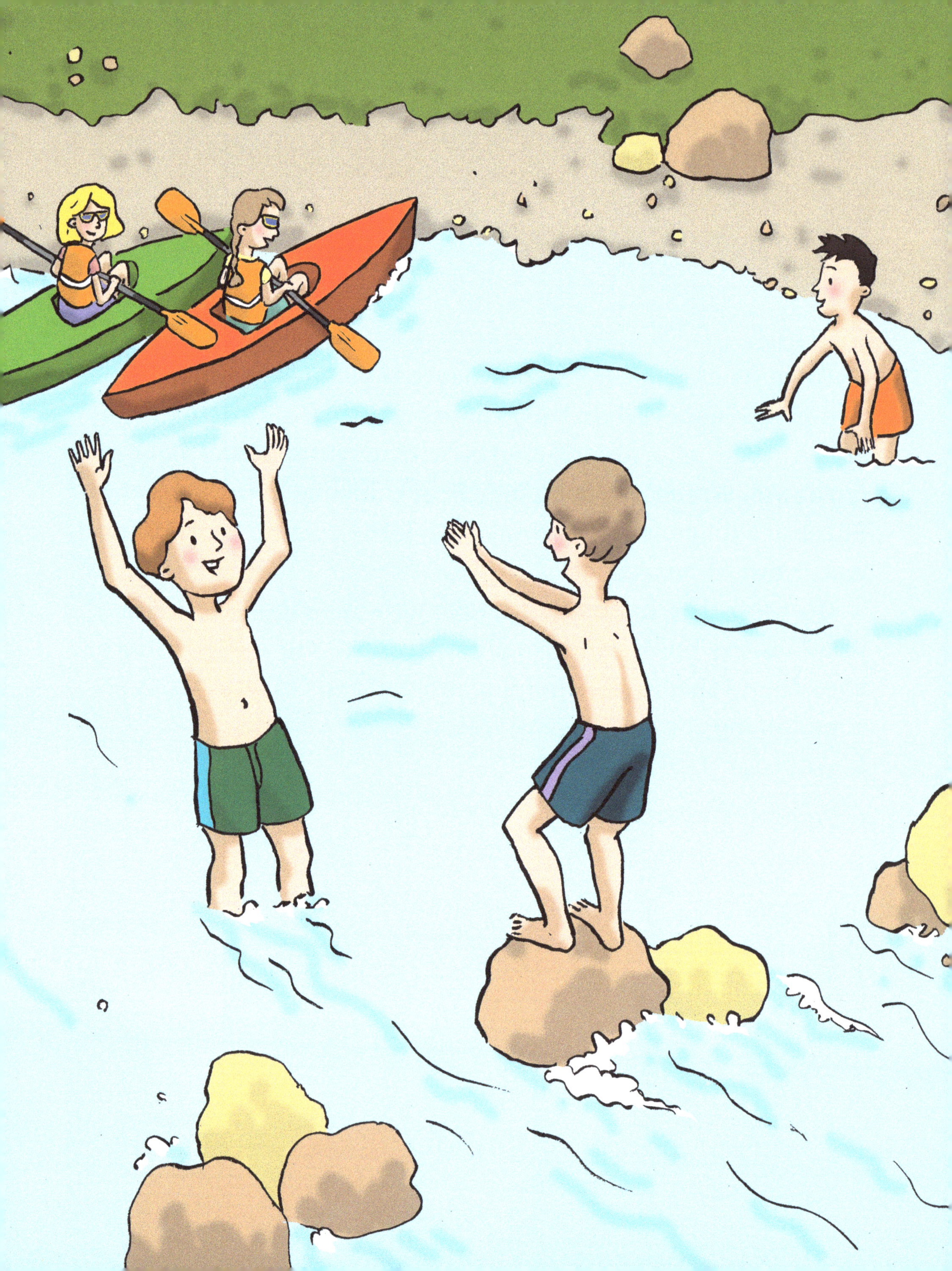

Elizabeth told her brothers about her leaky kayak as they played in the water together.

"Is that what took you so long?!" Christopher asked. "We decided that you must have fallen into the water!"

"Course not," retorted Elizabeth." We didn't even get dumped in the rapids."

Christopher's funny half grin made Abigail suspicious. "Did you get dunked?" she asked him.

It was the boys' turn to tell how Chris's kayak had overturned shooting the rapids. The girls felt quite smug because their record was still better than their brothers'.

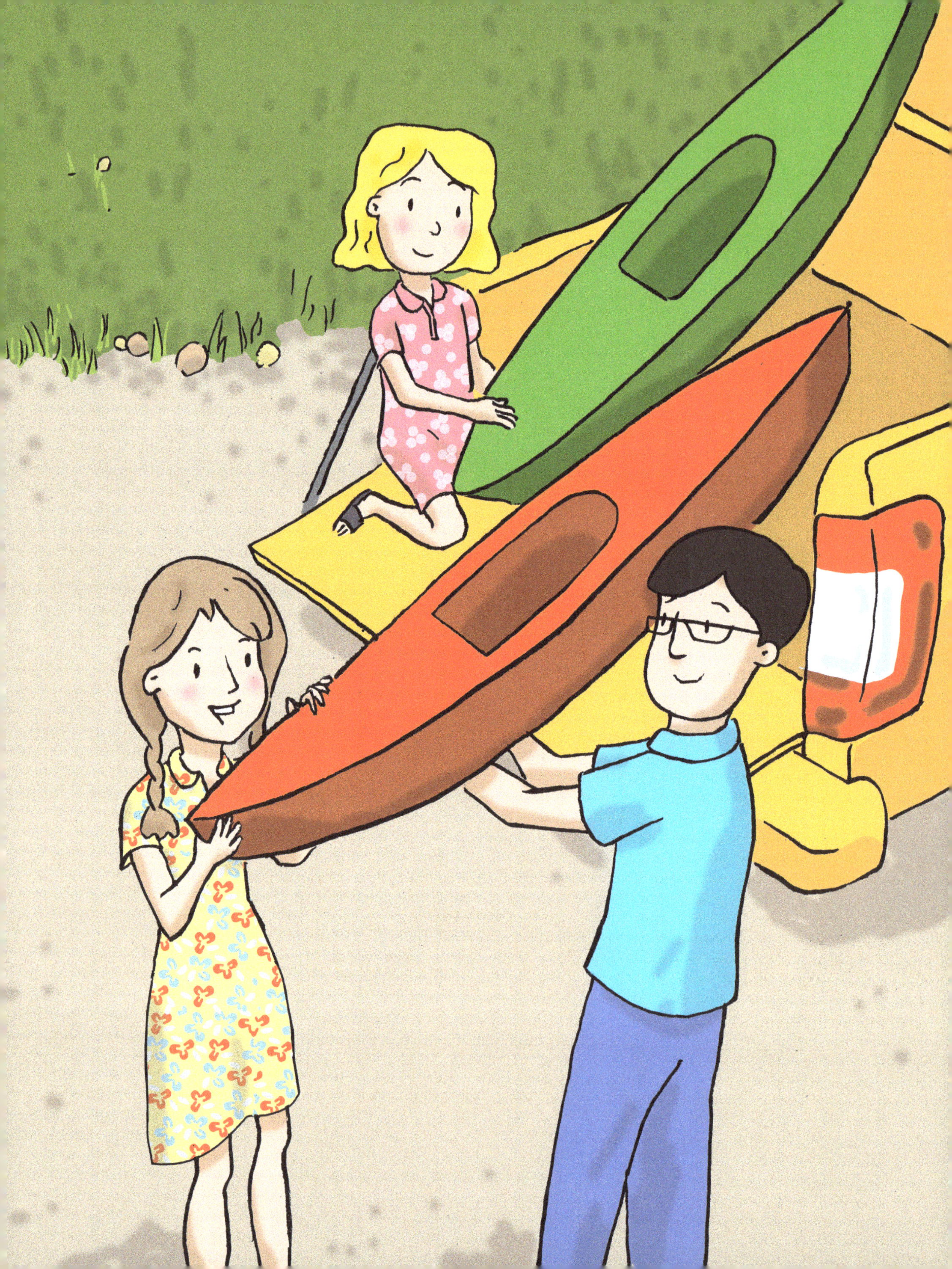

All too soon Dad's pickup pulled up, and everyone helped to load the kayaks. They headed back to the cabin tired but happy and very hungry. Elizabeth rode in the back with the kayaks, the breeze drying her clothes.

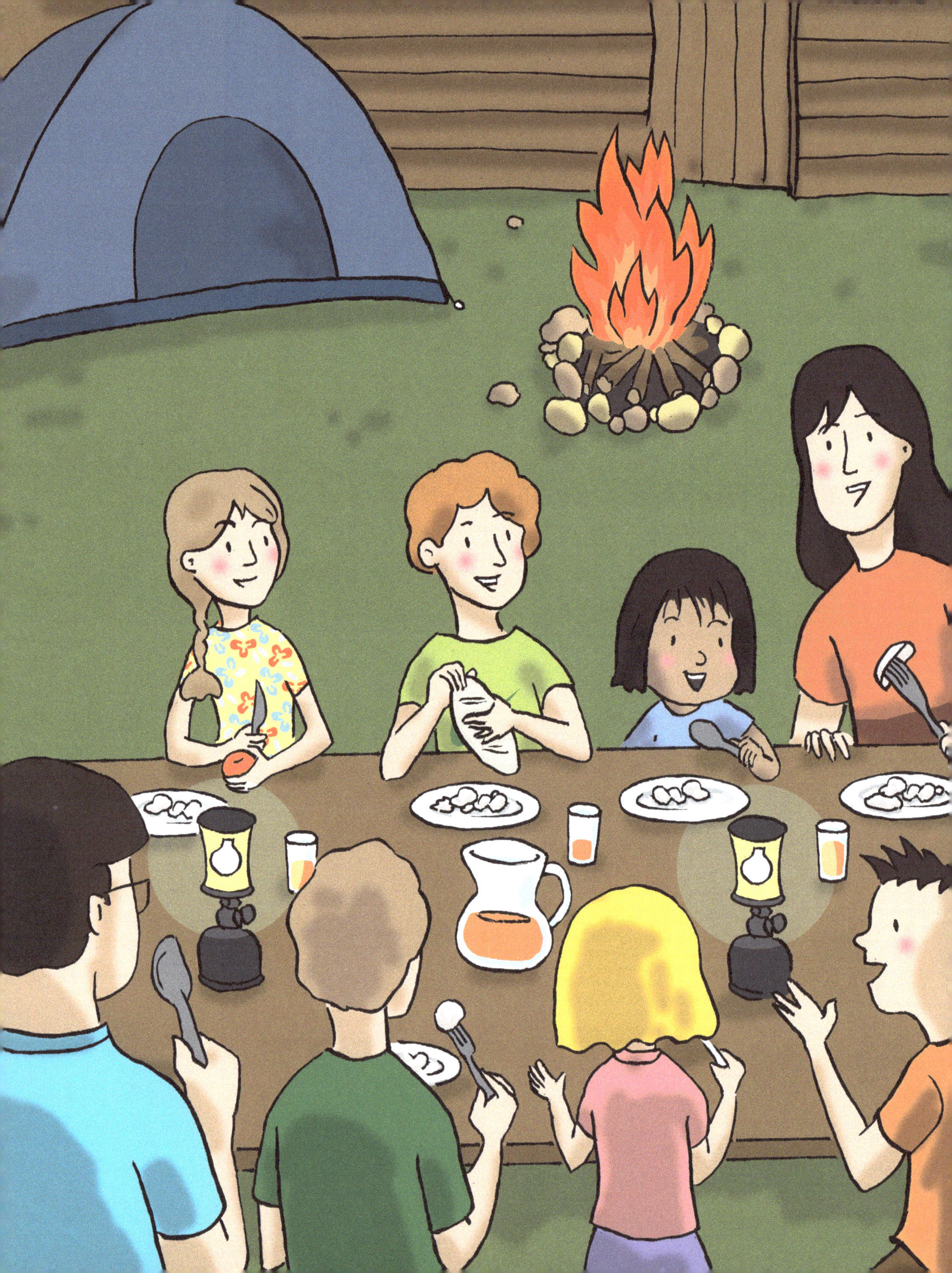

The BBQ chicken smelled so good when they got back to their campsite. No one needed any urging to gather around the picnic table to eat. Chips, watermelon, and some of Dad's yummy grilled chicken. It couldn't get better than that!

Later, as they gathered around the fire roasting marshmallows and making s'mores, the fireflies rose above the meadow grasses like confetti. The stars came out, one by one, and the full moon rose big and orange over the treetops.

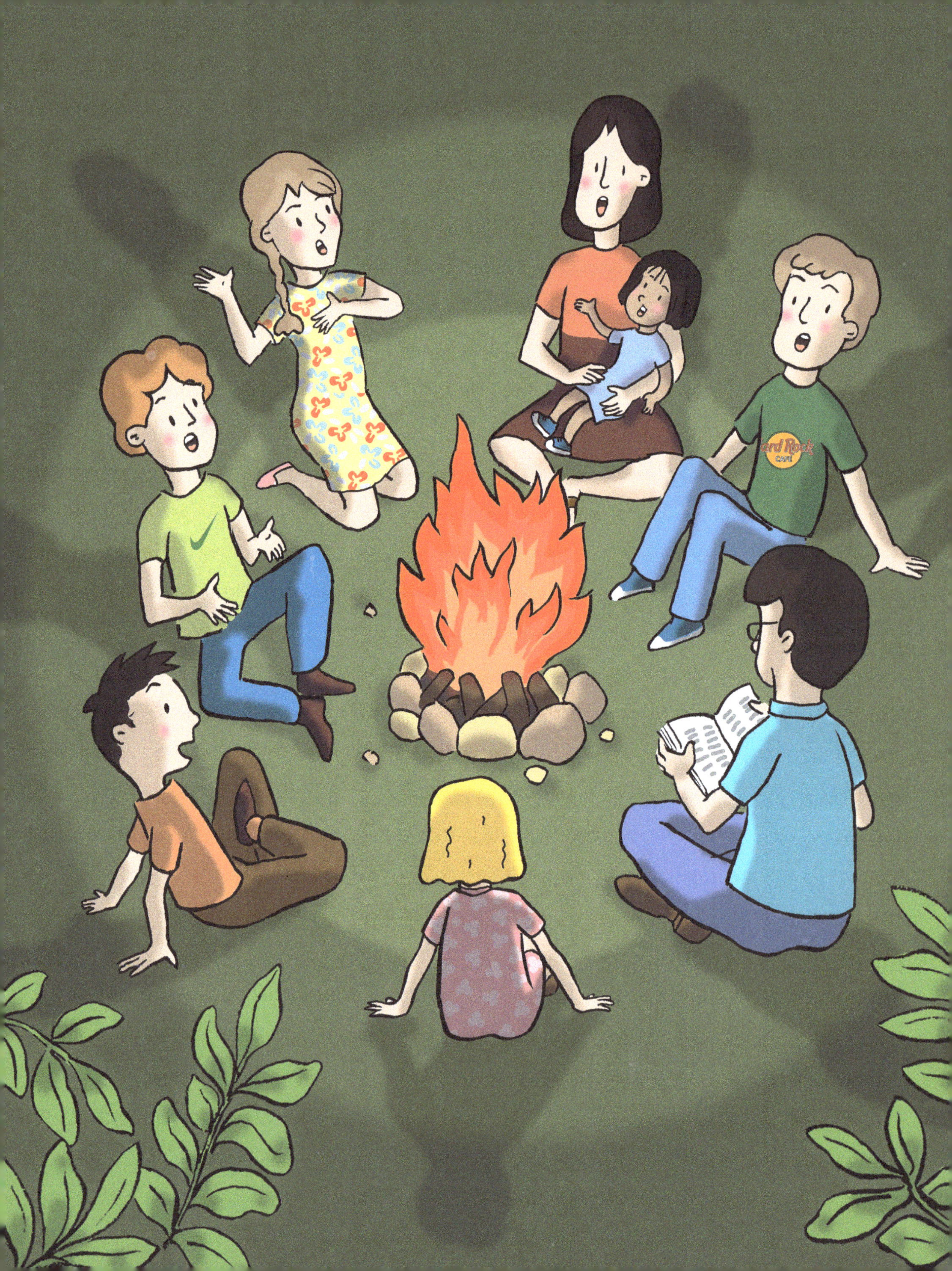

Dad read a few Scripture verses, and they all sang some songs. After the prayer, Mom and Victoria headed for the cabin. Elizabeth and Abigail cleaned up after supper, and they all headed for bed.

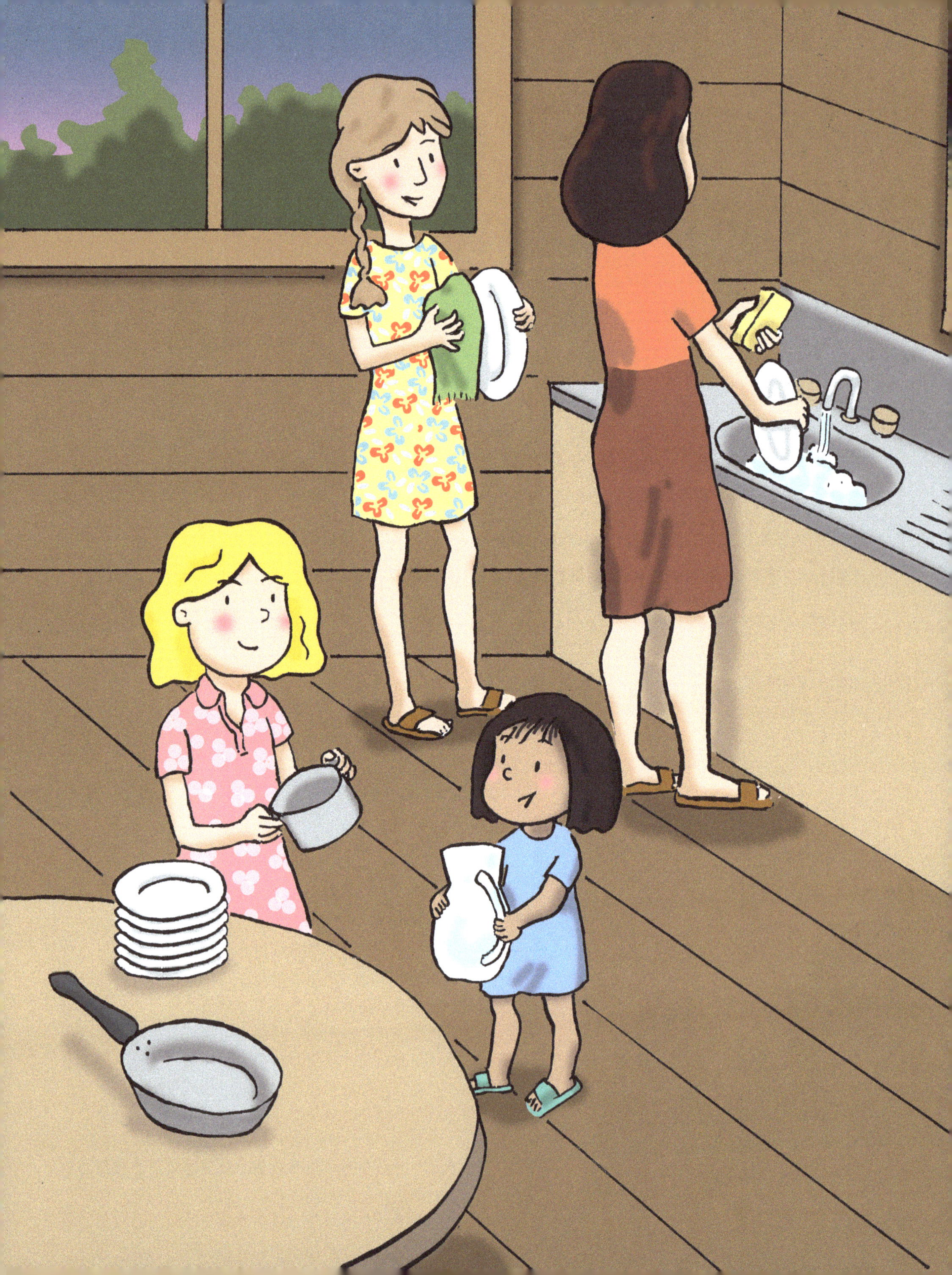

Their weary muscles were aching, and their sunburned skin was a reminder to the campers that they should have used their sunscreen before they headed out today. They crawled into their sleeping bags in the tent, and it wasn't long until they were all in dreamland.

ICE CREAM

The family camping trip was always the highlight of the summer. The hike to the waterfalls, biking down to the little ice cream shop for cones, fishing, and the yummy fish fry for supper in the evening. Those activities were all an important part of the family's tradition. It was always sad when it ended.

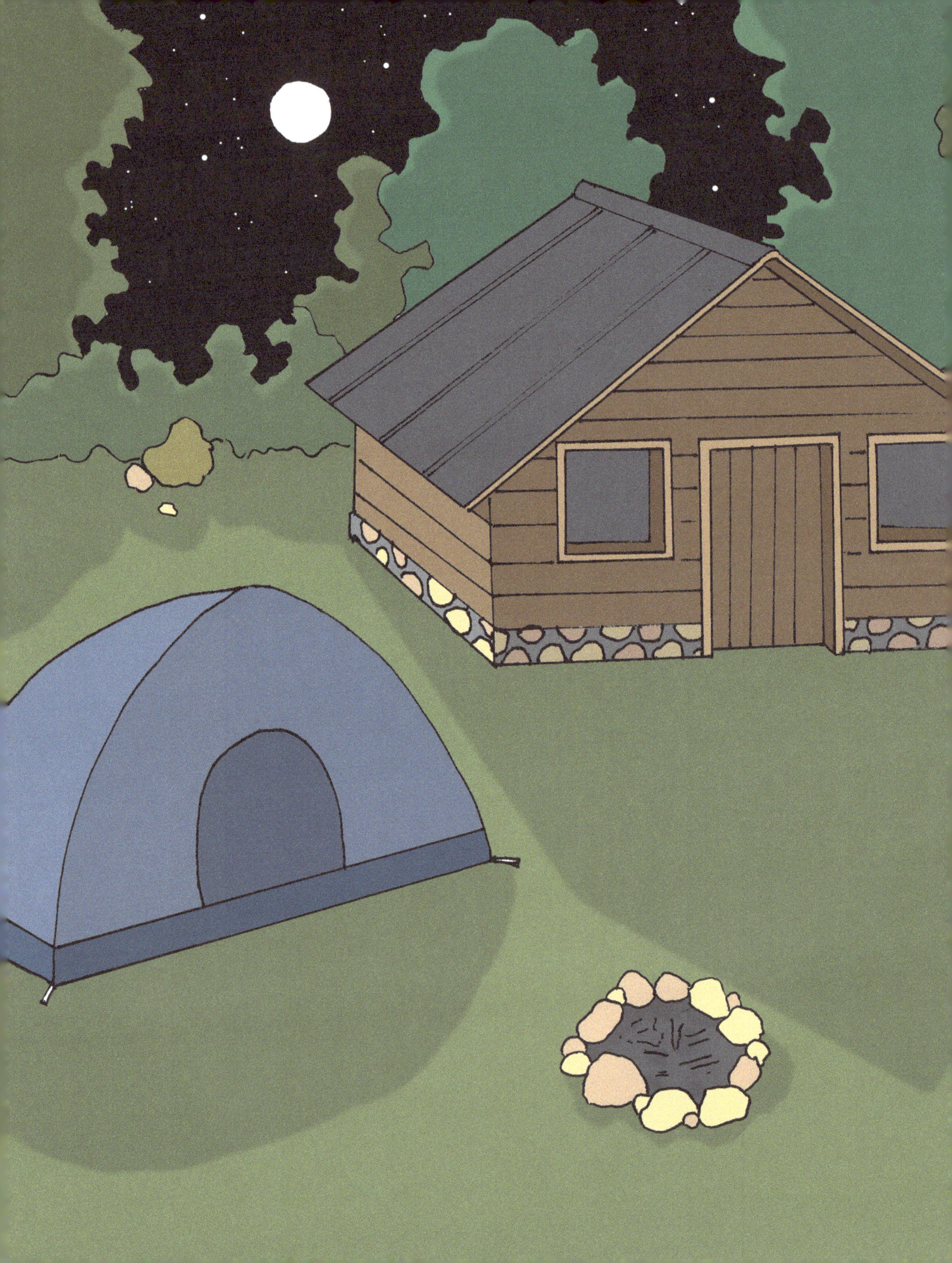

The next day, they packed up their gear, and loaded their things onto the Gator and the four-wheeler. They headed out to where their vehicles were parked. Although they were all sad to leave, Elizabeth was already looking forward to their time at the cabin next summer.

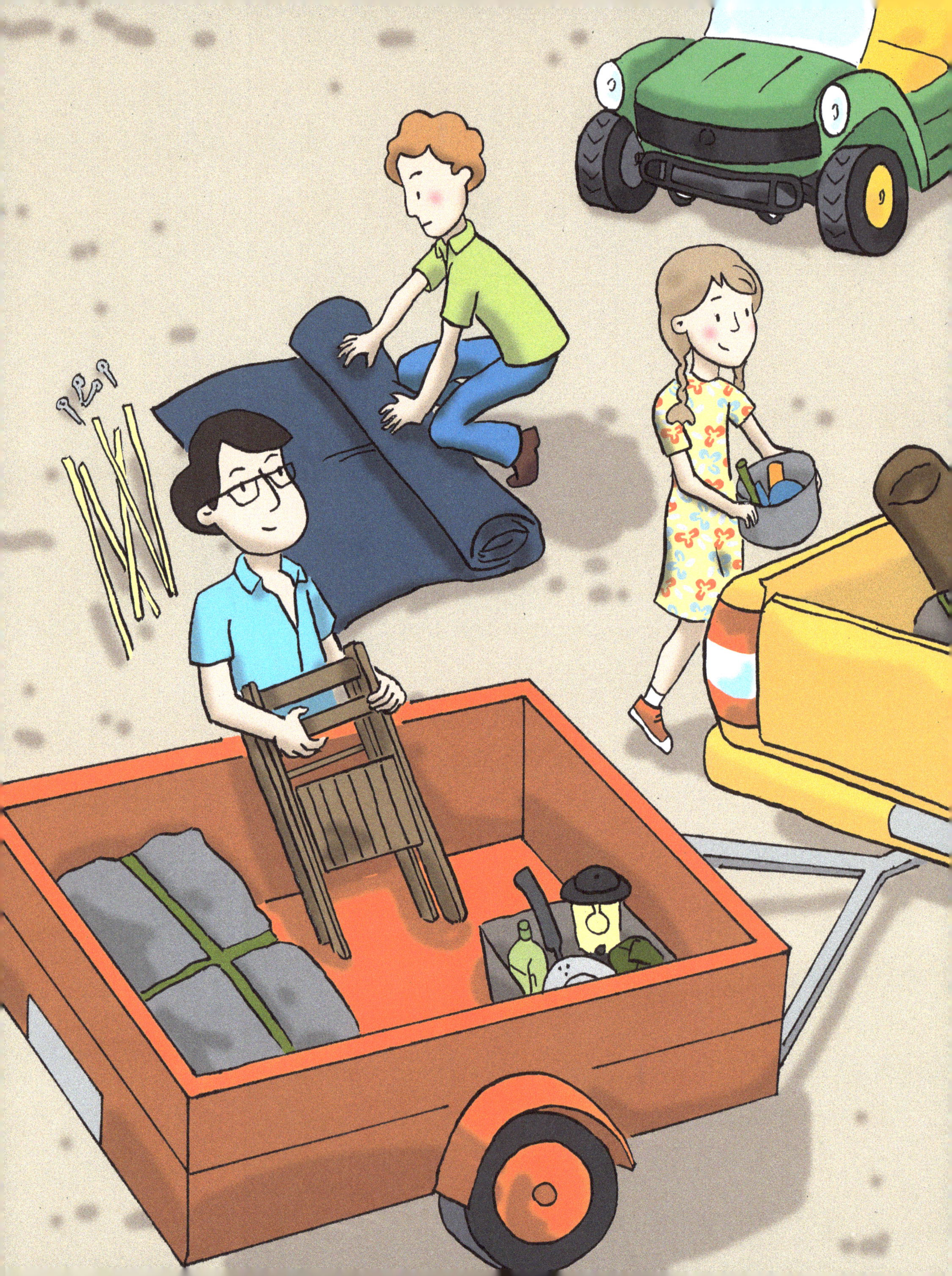

As they were riding, Elizabeth remembered seeing the beaver swimming in the river the one evening after supper. Benjamin had thrown a rock close to the beaver, so they could see and hear the beaver slap its tail on the water before it dove to safety.

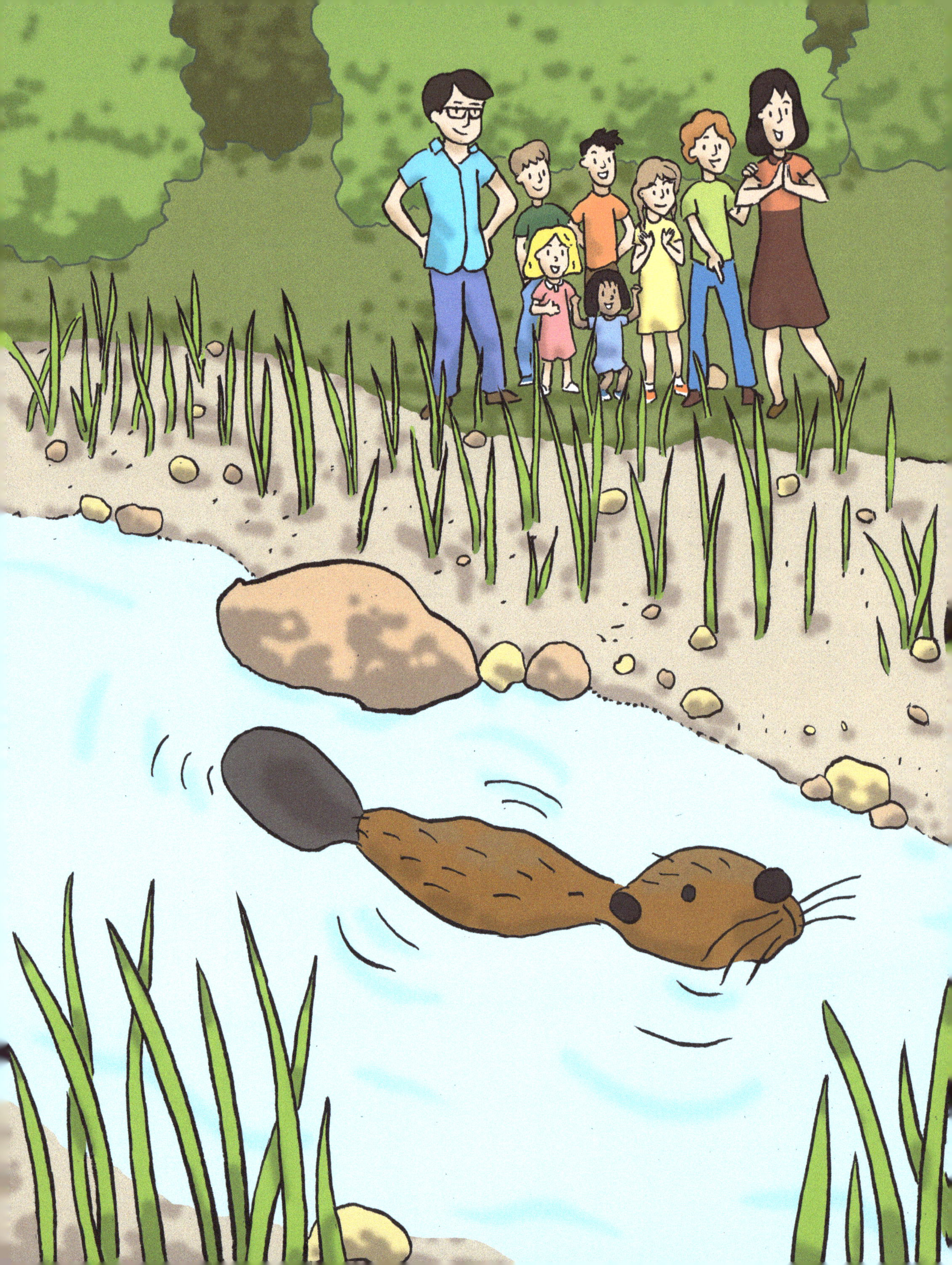

It wasn't unusual to spot a bear on the drive to the cabin. But this year, they'd set a record for the most bears they had ever seen. Six in all. Well, at least Mom, Dad, and Nicholas had seen six. The rest had only seen five, but that was still more than the usual two or three.

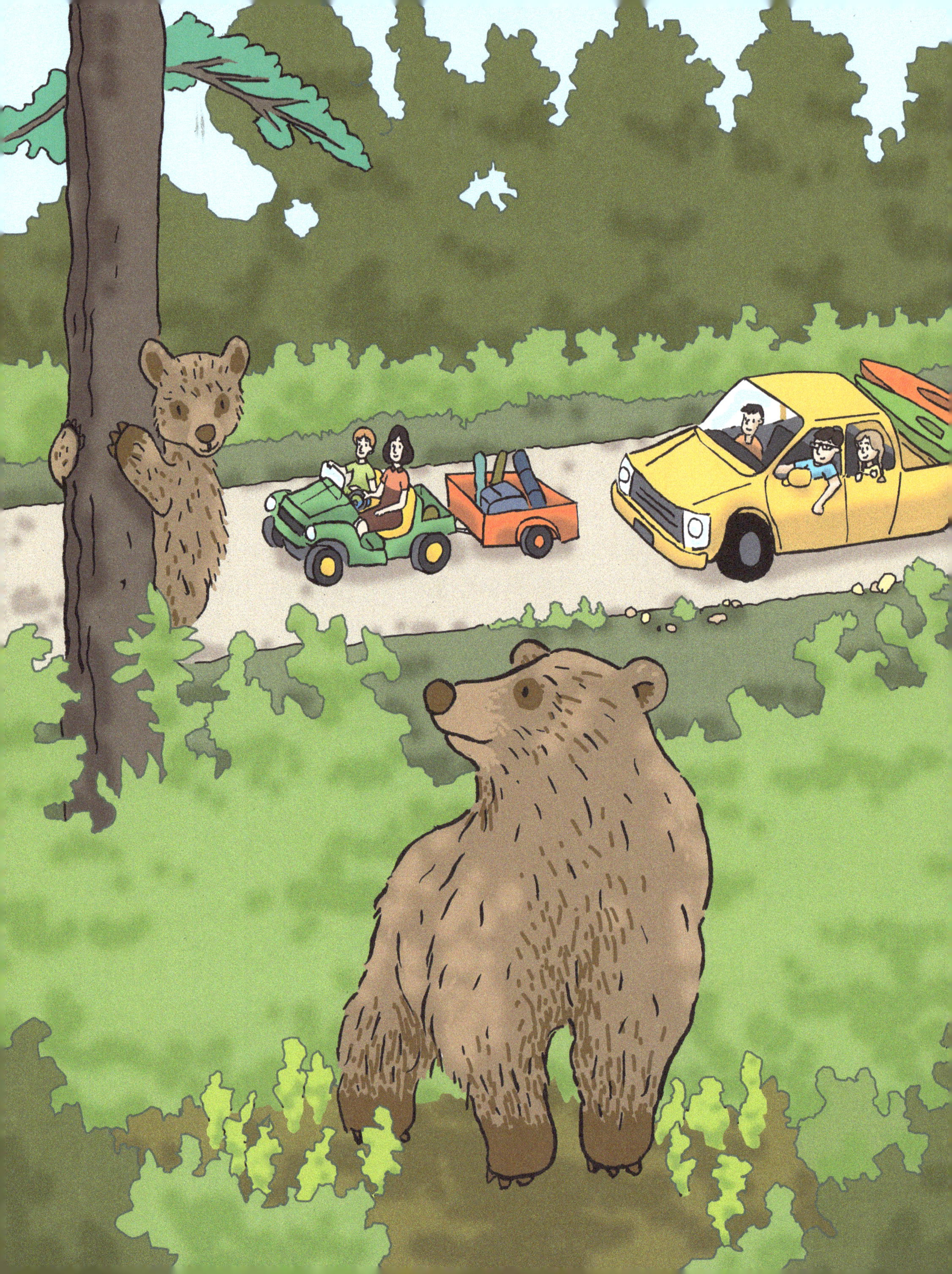

Elizabeth was startled back to reality by Abigail's cry of dismay. She had lost her cell phone! It was nowhere to be found! Somehow, it must have jiggled out of her pocket when they drove over the rough sections of the trail.

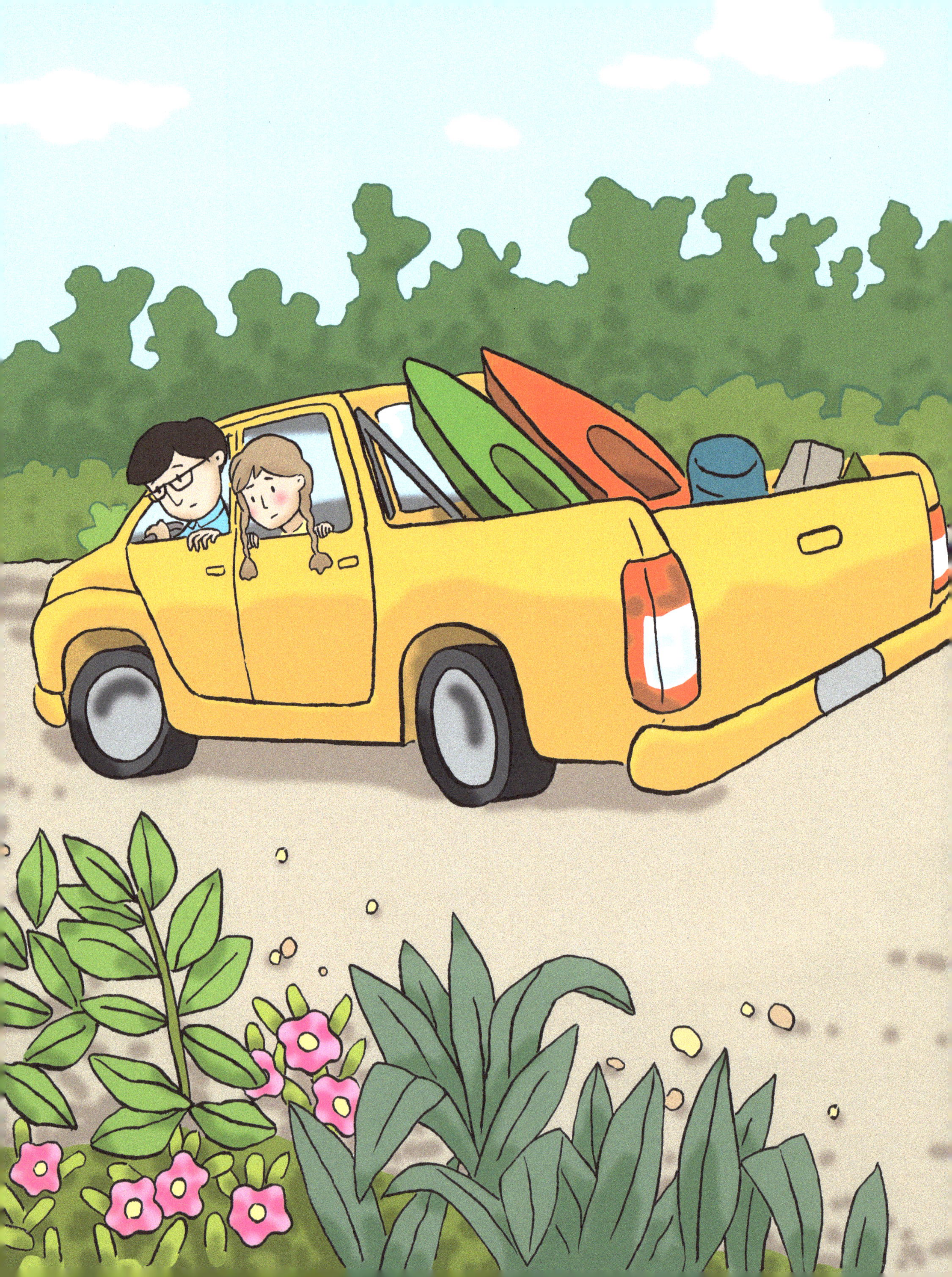

As they turned around to go look for it, Elizabeth prayed to God for help. It felt almost pointless to look–it was like looking for a needle in a haystack. Would God care enough about a phone to show them where it was?

They drove slowly back the way they'd come, scanning both sides of the trail. A quarter of a mile back, they went through a washout from a recent rain.

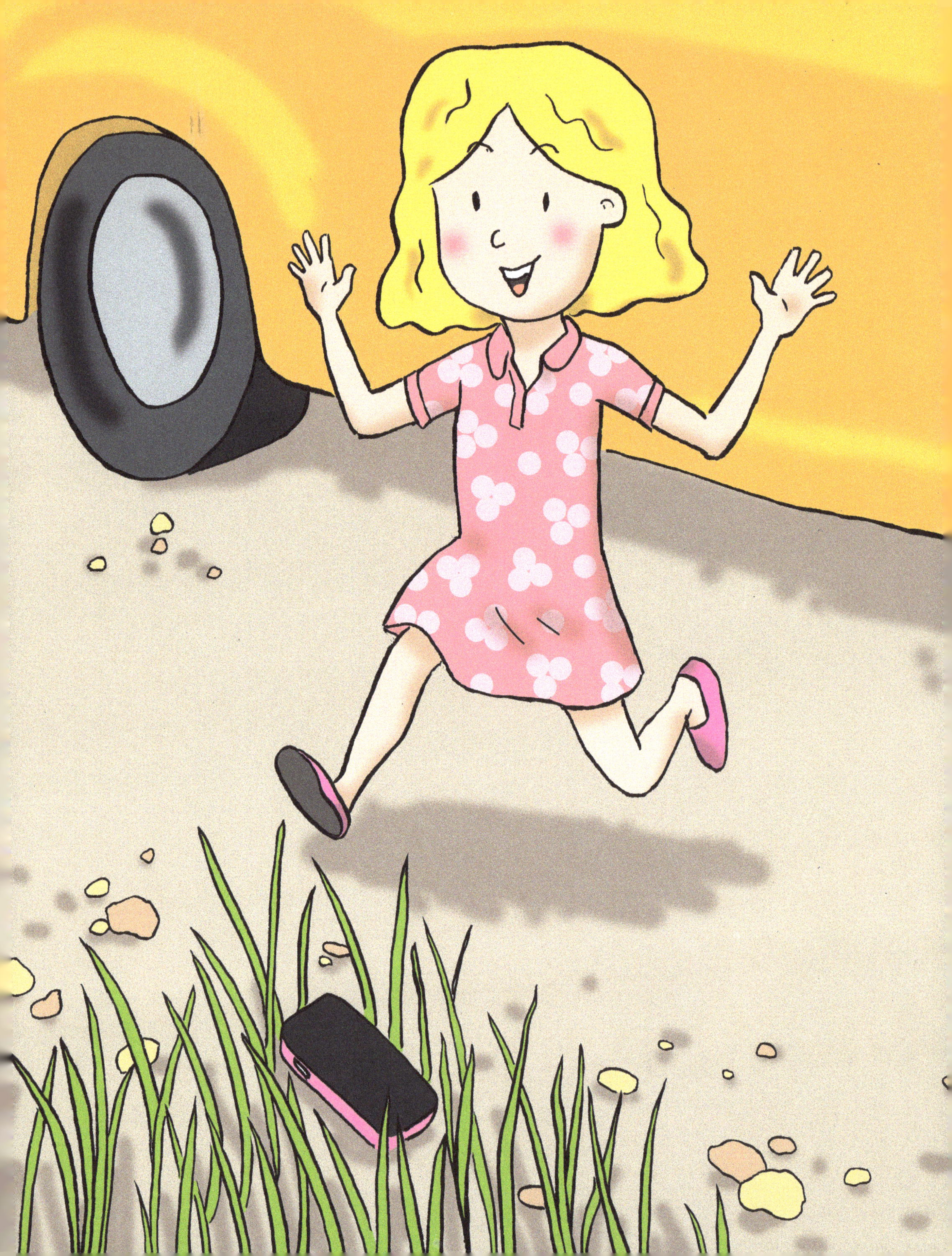

Right there, lying faceup on the path was the phone, just waiting for them to find it.

Abigail hopped off the Gator to retrieve it. Apparently when they'd jolted through the dip earlier, it was enough of a bump to make her phone slide out of her pocket without her even realizing it.

With grateful hearts, they turned around and headed back to the pickup once again. Elizabeth sent up a silent thank you to God for caring enough to help them find her sister's phone.

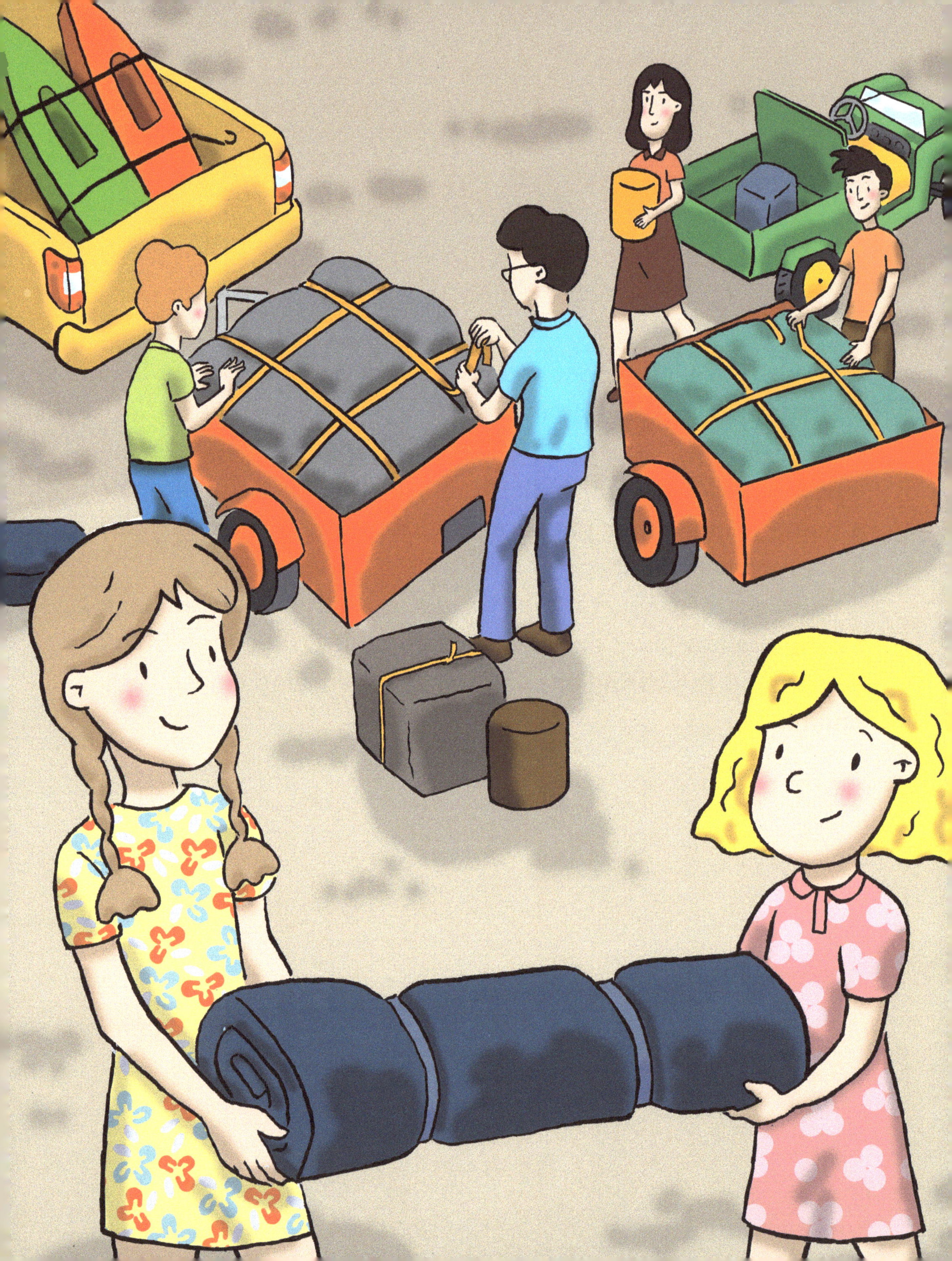

Remembering God's promise, Elizabeth whispered the Bible verse, "before thou callest on me, I will answer from Heaven!"

The same God who had made this beautiful world for them to enjoy also loved them so much that He answered their prayer for help.

They had called and He had answered just like He promised he would. What a mighty God we serve!

CPSIA information can be obtained
at www.ICGtesting.com
Printed in the USA
LVHW072210191022
730974LV00039B/63

9 780228 877141